Dusk:
New and Selected Poems

Dusk:
New and Selected Poems
I.P. Taylor

Smokestack Books
1 Lake Terrace, Grewelthorpe, Ripon HG4 3BU
e-mail: info@smokestack-books.co.uk
www.smokestack-books.co.uk

ISBN 9780995563575

Smokestack Books is represented
by Inpress Ltd

to Rosi,
a constant source of
encouragement through the years

Contents

High Intake

The house was half-sunk in the nettlebed.

Among cobwebs like the shadows
of storm-torn curtains,
among the dried-up husks of rats,
the dark pulse had ached,
while the place sundered under the wind.

The world stepped back from the door,
left the three of them alone.

Peatcutters hunched past,
their eyes fixed to the heather,
heard the dogs' rage after vermin
at the back of the bat-hung barn,
muttered and glanced back
when they'd ten minutes' space between them.

Roadsters, flapping like lame crows,
crossed the brown moor
under the white sky,
saw the girl at the pump handle
turn a face pale as firstlight,
but would not sup at the well
or stop in the lee of the farm's walls.

An occasional rider, his brain
racing like a moor hare, passed
in a low mist at evening, bent
at speed, his eyes to the track,
heard the woman's screams
as if a demon flayed her...

In a spring of high wind
and high water the man died
from a dose enough for all his vermin,
taken away unmourned on a cart, leaving
his work clothes to be burned,
his best boots to be sold.

The wild journeyman surprised asleep
in the loft stayed a week, cut wood,
mended the roof and the chimney,
built up the walls round the field
and took the girl with him,
while the woman slept
with the feel of him still within her...

The tinkers came in the summer,
found the chained dogs' bones
in the yard and the woman swaying
in the barn's draughts –

Took the axe they cut her down with.

When Beasts Most Graze

1

left their houses weeping and became unemployed
and finally... died in poverty
and so ended their days

(Commission of Inquiry Returns, 1517)

Tenant at Will, Wharram Percy (c.1500):

They found me at Milndam, at the fish pond,
the landmaster's men. They said
Leave your nets, William. We're fishers of men.
Come with us to the Lord's house. Come,
and receive the Word.
                                I followed,
sharp as a fox out of cover. Squire Hilton
hung like a cloud on his front step.
His smile axed at my heart.
He gave me till Michaelmas –
'Tell the whole village the same.'

I looked up to the furlongs, the skyline
of corn. I heard children laugh
by the stream. I turned from his gate.
For Hilton a sheep-run.
For the cottar death with the plough.

Our young men wanted to fight, but
I counselled acceptance: To sever one stoat
will summon the pack. We have no rights here,
leave behind little. Our tears
like our toil will fade into the land...

We gathered below Town Field.
Swallows twitched from the church tower,
bellied the shallows. Next year
they'll nest in the houses, singing
to idle spindles and empty hearths.

2

for where there have been a great many householders
and inhabitants there is now but
a shepherd and his dog
(Bishop Latimer, 1549)

Shepherd of Wharram Percy (c.1501):

Wharram, Octon, Bartindale, Argam
gone – choked under wool. What weighs
more than a bag o' wheat?
Why, man – a bleat!

I'm lucky, I know. I've moved
to this fine stone house that was William's.
The others are down. The best timbers gone
for the Hall, the rest for the sheep fence.

Last September groped by like a blind hag.
Most cursed the shepherd, many
the priest. Hilton had need of us both.
Like rabbits we kept to our doors.

I watched them, threading away
down the valley. Bent like a wind-whipped thorn,
the priest wept alone in the church.
I crept the Manor lawns, waiting Hilton's command.

whither shall they go?
– forth from shire to shire
and to be scattered thus abroad...
by compulsion driven some of them
to beg and some to steal
(Sheep Pamphlets)

Former Cottar of Wharram Percy:

On the Wolds' slopes distrust.
In the towns rejection. At Grimston
mute cottagers stared. In Malton
they barred the doors. To York,
William said: There'll be work.
Shelter. A larger place will seclude us.

But in York there were many like us
and a threatening fear among townsmen.
Some of us left for the coast. In our camp
by the Derwent old William failed.
We fashioned a hurdle, then Thomas
and I bore him back to the village...

In William's cottage the shepherd slept,
thick as a mole under a clod. We hunched
in a doorway. Cold chiselled our bones.
As first-light dusted the hills the slight breathing
stopped. We built a low cairn for the body,
our words too stubborn for prayer.

4

But I fancy that the town
has been eaten up with time,
* poverty, and pasturage*
(Abraham de la Pryme,1697)

Wharram Percy in recent times:

If you ask in the parish they'll tell you the way –
unless they're keepers. Press them,
and they'll say it was taken by plague...

Come in July to the dig. Learn of the finds
that jog a response to the pulse of the place:
the pair of dice, the bone needle, a thimble,
a coin...
                    Or come in spring
when the form of the land is most easily seen:

Fasten your boots. For the last half mile
follow the hollow way. Descend between swallows
cresting the slopes of young corn.

The roofless church is alone in the valley
like an old jaw loose with decay.
To the west, on the scarp-edge,
are the humps of the houses,
shallow graves in the grass.

The earth lies quiet above them,
preserving a sadness restrained over time.

Ironstone Miners, 1874

They wound up the track,
only their boots' crunch
breaking the moor's silence.

The lockout had forged
new sinews: they tensed
as the gates swung back.

They stepped from dark to dark,
wading the swilling passages
three miles to the drift.

Returning, drenched, into
the blizzard's grip, their clothes
burdened them like a punishment.

Around the stoves they wrenched
their boots free, like offending limbs,
before the frost's teeth met.

Their silence total,
steady as their hate.

Their eyes pitched into the flames.

The Hollow Places

December afternoon:
                    the long contours
are tractorless, autumn routines
died back to stackyards.

                    Acid light eats
into woodsides. The western sky
aquamarine, air with the bite
of freshness before frost.
                    Ten miles north
snow-swirls trail from bulging cumulus…

                    A lithe breeze,
lean as a weasel, rakes the matted grass
that masks the rubble of Tunnel Top.
The holly that scratched the gable
hisses alone in the wind.
                    Tyremarks
in the mud and a vandalised branch –
Christmas has come.

Woodland shadows flood east,
blotting the cottage sites…

                    *

Like an underwater amphitheatre
Tunnel Wood glows gold-green.

                    Where the slope
levels, below beech-depth,
the old tunnel drips.
                    Springs squirm
through the chalk and vanish
into blackness.

                    Toss a rock
in the openmouthed smoke-vent –
wake the last call.

                    *

The vision gripped them
till the cash ran out.
                    Companies,
underestimating time, flexed
against the chalk and fell.
                    Two hundred men
roared from their hillside bothies,
split skulls against pickshafts…

                    But the tunnel
won its dynamited mile – obsolete
within a century.

                    *

                    Sunlight
coppers the horizon, dusts
the ploughland with a russet haze…

                    From the bank top
the green road's pre-Roman line
backbones the wold.
                    Its thorn-fringe
claws in like beggars.
                    Here
a stony link half ploughed, to add
an acre to the barley crop –
the terminal invasion.

                    *

After the horse days, labourers drained
from the wold.
                    Ambitious farms
fattened in the tractor's wake,
annexed the lands of smaller neighbours,
watched the old homes erode –
spectres against the light.

                    A mile west
the hulk of Wold House juts
from its sea of winter wheat,
the gaping centre of a single field
the reach of the old farm's boundary.

                    The ruin
yawns across a shallow riffling sea,
a hangar for the wind.

                    Clouds
bandage the sunset. Gusts
nag the hands, like young dogs
impatient to move on.

                    *

At the fork, the green road slumps
under tarmac.
                    Its lands impressed
Vessey Pasture huddles behind the trunks
of a threadbare larch-break. Grass hangs
from the eaves like stalactites –
the parasites are sleepless…

                    *

Drains glaze…

A sludge of ice
thickens in ruts, the furtive stiffening
that tightens toward dusk.

Fences strewn
like bones, the ploughmen's crofts
at Swinham shoulder the chalk scarp
to the plain.
Wood pigeons burst
from the lofts like missiles...
Wind has forestalled
stoical weekenders, bared
the structure to the ribs.

*

Curtains
of hail draw in. Shadows
flap into the woods.
Fields darken,
their spurious bloom burned out.

Night seeps over the wold,
closes like Usher's tarn
over the tokens that remain.

Stormed

The windows glimpsed it as it sprang –
they stared back stiff as victims.

A wingspread fell across the room
like a prophecy fulfilled.

Light shrank to a gash. Wind
beat the eves like dull artillery.

Beneath the thunderheads horizon lightning
bobbed like a fevered dream. Trees
staggered there – refugees
from the streaming night clutching their loads.

Dawn was white,
late,
drained.

Inch by inch sounds
squeezed out, to twitch
like severed nerves,
testing air for reassurances –

The taut resetting of normality.

Kelly

Loose-jawed as a goat,
he grinned at neighbour and stranger
without discrimination. Words
had been long abandoned,
dumped in the hedgeback
as decisively as worn-out boots.

He needed none for cats.
The saddle room grate boomed
like a smithy, veteran toms
in mute expedient truce, circled
his feet like coils of energy,
eager for feed in the log blaze.

He hoed the big fields on the Wolds' farms:
summer nights in the field barns,
in winter the strawlofts, rank
with labourers' sweat. The wind
gnawed out his ears, left the husks
clung like dead leaves.

They dug his age from the Atlantic bog
and gave him a pension. He retired
to one side of the stackyard, lugged
a tonnage of larch trunks from the windbreaks,
lean as a mountain warrior,
a spray of white hair in the wind.

He outlived them all,
those wild Wold Rangers: Paddy
and Smiler, inebriate Lydia;

The last of the old itinerants,
gone from the crop fields
like skylarks from the heath...

The saddle room roof has fallen now
and the cats have gone somewhere warmer.

Bat Poem

I began like a row of beautiful white notes
played once and sealed perfect.

But my hands sprawled across them
in a dream
and the sound broke
deep wounds in my face.

Now I crawl beams
like a gob of night,
a chill shudder at dusk for gnats.

The ticking beetle rots floors through my sleep –
my night opens in a defecation of moth skulls.

Behind the rent of my flight
the moon claws up her eastern rope.

I am as cold as moonwash –
the serrated edge of fear.

I have no voice for love.

I am safe so long as I don't change.

Blackamore

1

Rage-haunt of gales

rampart of summit bog
and rock silence

refuge of exiles
deprived migrations

tomb of toiled landscapes

layered millennia
of abandoned clan-worlds

2

Oar-flash in the bay
iron swords on the headland –

a flood-tide muffled by grass

wind-borne distance:
a stipple of cries
like the soots of wings

the north yawns over them –

a supplanted culture

flint blade
urn bones
sunk under the ridge

moor soil is acid
herdsmen of the Celtae

3

Cerialis

Agricola

the Levisham lords
harnessed to squalor

Brigantian hopes spattered
before Stanwick

stone setts
coast forts

mercenary defenders

causeways of slain

4

A snapped axle: its skyward wheel
milling flailed hoof-dust

the ghost of a charioteer
curls off the cornland

a clash of farmers

dependence or death –
a Saxon is adamant

moor soil is acid
sheep flocks of the Danelaw

5

Bottle-glass twilight under the conifers

a generation of fences
wildfires

still we come
to rest eyes on the heather

to touch something deeper:

enigma of standing stone
and tumulus

hollow ways
ridge trods

whispers of spirits
in abandoned byre and bield

Holocaust

A month's drought:
east winds wither the land;
earth cracks, every ridge
is a thousand dried-out mouths...

A straggle of Sunday hikers
threads the moor. The peat-scab
breaks: Sahara dry, its dust
spews from insouciant boots.

Laughter of disregard:
a black fan opens
from a tidalwave of flame...

The moor inverts its image
in the sky: a desert sunset
shocked into midday dusk.

Beneath it men lose hair,
eyebrows, shirts. A fire tender,
caught in a tortured curve of flame,
shatters like a land mine.

Sheep, hares, foxes panic upwind,
stampeding to clear air. They burst
from the blaze like brands:
streaks of terror, incandescent.

Haze thickens. The sky is a sandstorm,
battle-brown. Heath peels faster
than a man can run. Peat burns inward,
a shimmering inferno twelve feet down.

The forestry erupts. Bulldozers
smash tracks through spruce. Peat
burns under them, trunks flare again.
The digger crews move in…

The conflagration is contained. The peat
is a roasting quicksand. It smoulders
like a lavaspread –
the deceptive mask of hell.

Grouse, curlew, plover, dip
above their offsprings' crematorium:
a five-mile tract of carcasses.

Farmers sell off the remnants
of their flocks: the commons an ashpit,
dead for fifteen years...

Surveillance is maintained. Danger
could break again before the rain.

Roads are closed: car jams
and cameras turned back.

The watchers wait for cloud.

Years

We use thought to protect ourselves from pain. What cannot be thought pierces us where we are weakest.
(Gabriel Josipovici)

Scrayingham: 1807

The trees raged, naked. But then they found
their god. They bend at the river's lip
and drink, tranquil. I, John Schorey,
grovel in the meads: a kneeling darkness,
my own headstone. I cannot ring the bells,
stand in the lighted porch, compel
my emptiness bid welcome. Mary,
dearest wife, why do you call? Why drag
my absence from the grass? Why weep
for one so long dead as I?

Scarborough Spa: 1807

All but the double voice, the breathing
of the sea – its boom and hiss –
has left me. I am a shell cast
from the ebb: echo of an echo.
Press me to your ear, Mary –
hear how the surface roars.
It is tears and laughter,
despair and hope. No cure
here. The deeps are soundless:
let prayer begin there.

Scarborough Spa: 1808

What can I say now that
will not oppress? That I have
stepped beyond the lamp's gleam,
found the room I thought certain
strange? Stone-mouthed men stand
at the door. You smile and say
'John, I shall visit you.' My love,
the space between us here is more
than the length of England. Its measure
is the stretched cry of my soul.

York Asylum: 1809

Leave me the silver timekeeper that nests
above your heart. It is a pledge
for my return. Observe, Mary,
its unpresuming prayer at noon.
It shall dwell against the vortex
of my grief – to sign me home.
Yield and endure. Waiting is
ample praise. Thundersquall and tempest
will pass across the meads, leaving
a valley patient again for rain.

Scrayingham: 1809

You close the casement. What was it
that you saw? The ghosts of willows?
Spectral wings upon the river?
You turn a face spent of reassurances.
We cannot speak. We are mourners
at each other's graves. You stoop away
through gardens of the past,
where flowers have petrified. I drift
back to my body in the cell –
a face trying to outstare eternity.

York Asylum: 1810

I have learned much of this affliction:
the chained are legion – their torment
saturates the air. I retch against
my very breath, surfeited on loss.
There are some here whose only solace
is to flay those scourged enough.
But know, Mary, whatever marks I bear
are the heart's wounds disfiguring the skin.
Do not protest. The keenest edge
I feel is the sting of my crippled soul.

York Asylum: 1812

What did they tell you, Mary? That sight
of me now would derange thought until
it burst the brain? Do the weak rave thus?
How long, my love, since you stood racked
within this room? The watch is gone –
taken by those who value metal
by its name. I sprawl like offal
on this Augean floor, a river's shift
from Scrayingham. Will God admit nothing?
What strength, what love, upholds me now?

Before You Turn Away

The eating eat
and the hungry wait
and the day comes again
whole
like a gift left just opened

*

He must have walked from the village
to pluck the last leaves from the bushes

He must have crawled on
or fallen
trapped between earth and sky

At the edge of the desert famine abandoned him
like a hard-eyed opportunist
and went back for his children

*

The rich stay rich
and the poor stay poor

The rich get richer
and the poor stay poor

The rich get poorer
and the poor get poorer

That lie grows fatter
but the poor stay poor

*

I sit in the prison of my bones
watching the heathaze
where my father searches

From horizon to horizon emptiness
the dimensions of a belly

My mother was buried in the mass grave
of official statistics

Kwashiorkor and Marasmus are my brothers

*

The eating eat
and the hungry wait
and the day comes again
without discrimination

Innocent as a babe awakening

Falklands, 1982

Again and again they keep on returning:
the ships and the servicemen
from the South Atlantic.

They have to keep coming back
for ever. They have to keep filling
our TV screens with heroes.

The government needs them
in place of a morality.

The people need them,
in place of an identity.

The nationalist psychology needs them,
like a junkie,
to get to tomorrow.

They keep on coming back
so we are never allowed to forget
the face of the god we serve.

So we are never allowed to arrive
at the end of the sentence.

Looking For Scotland

1

Because of Culloden and Clearances

Because of supermarkets and central heating

Because of our need to reconnect
with deeper realities

This is, as the blurb says,
the last great wilderness area in Europe.

I arrive among drizzle and midges, Tourist Board
and NTS images filling the windscreen,
displacing the eyes.

I snoop for a while with the cruising saloons
of the property cult: Swedes, Danes,
Germans, prospecting the loch shores,
hungry to buy up the unknown.

From the holiday bungalow's picture-postcard windows
the wilderness almost greets me.

I step into it, across the new red tarmac...

2

No footpath here now to the croft's spilled walls:

Storm-scattered turf stacks,
bald black pads in the grass
like abandoned bootsoles.

Generations of silence among the bog cotton…

Inside its fleece a dead sheep rots
like the old clan fabric
under absentee leaders.

Broadsword and plaid, pipers and pride,
sold to the unaware by the uncaring?

Furious ghosts glare out
from brochures and beleaguered battlements,
as the indelible earth still wakes us
with blood-soaked betrayals.

Silence in the bog cotton,
each fallen stone an indictment...

3

A fugitive moon skulks behind cloud,
a Bonnie Prince Charlie moon.

Otters follow the loch shore:
a silhouette-flow against night-tide
liquid on liquid.

If I'd been out to check nets
would I wait clutching a shotgun?

Beyond the need fire's circle of sanctity
in the disaffected darkness of the past
bloodied accusers crowd
awaiting justice,

As visions of the future –
that elusive unitive vision –
build and collapse
in the daylight's baleful embers.

So many Scotlands to fight for,
so many Scotlands forgotten:

Gusting spray at Glomach's edge
like blown hair of lost firstlove,

Faery singing fading on the wind.

The Old Ones

Donald, the youngest at seventy-nine,
went out early, with the fixed purpose
of a fanatic, to find the cow...
She could be anywhere within a mile,
lying like a red sandstone boulder
in the boggy pasture's whispering reeds.

Murdo was off too, on the eight miles
of rocky footpath to the village shop,
to queue for oats and tea
and discuss the world in monosyllables
with aging neighbours, checking
the temptation to indulge in a Mars bar.

Sandy worked on the big boat
his arthritis would not let him row,
keeping her caulked and painted
for the catch he would never make,
watching the veil of sea mist
lifting on Raasay like a revelation.

Between the batterings of Atlantic storms
on the corrugated roof Angus, the oldest
at ninety, kept up their resistance...
Fine afternoons he hoed their kitchen plot,
while the reeds, like a besieging army,
camped patiently on the pasture.

I used to go to collect the milk,
sit silent by the sweet peat fire
in the mellow peace of their breathing,
while Jeanie, their grand-niece, made tea,
hearing the tranquil tick of the grandfather clock
and the stags roaring on Skye and Raasay...

Coming back fifteen years on the house
was still standing but empty, their bible left
on the table as if they'd just gone up to bed...
Sandy's boat stripped like the skeletal ribs
of their old dead cow and the reeds
pressed up to the house wall.

And the silence it seemed
no longer peace, but desolation.

Toff

Oi, kid!

There were three of them:
crew cuts and tapered pants,
life-hardened eyes cold
as stream-washed stone,

voices raw as the gales
that raged on the moor edge,
hands tough as frost-split rock...

Oi, kid –
Let's 'ave a go on yer bike!

He couldn't escape, mesmerised
by the venom in those eyes,

watched them career through the market pens
taking turns, with whoops and yeehas,
like an impromptu rodeo...until
they'd wrecked his bike
and left, cursing his birth.

He stared at the mangled thing
lying there, like a storm-smashed bird,
that had once been gift-bright and perfect...

Through his shock,
his gate-post paralysis,
he felt he was somehow to blame
for a crime he could not remember –

not understanding
the handed-down legacy of hate,
the long oppressive centuries of pain.

At the Rock

Another Saturday night:
the streets around the dance hall
thronged as a mediaeval fair...

The Irish traveller lads arrived
to sing, like latter-day bards,
to grab the mic and roar out
Elvis and Jerry Lee, claiming
they were both from Donegal.

The local clan chiefs, leathered
and quiffed, lounged around the walls,
watching rival warbands form, probing
weaknesses like inveterate raiders.

The wild moor girls descended on the loos
like shrieking marsh demons,
pushing through, all big hips
and damp clits,
to grab an eyeful
a handful
or a quick screw in the cubicles...

As the warriors spilled outside
to boast and taunt
and exchange blows
the veterans emerged,
disdainful battle-champions,
to pick off the winners
take heads and maintain status...

Then through the bloody throng
swept Mandy, like the Morrigan,
tits first and focused,
to scoop a fresh young pup
to abduct for supper.

Scorned

He comes like the day trippers
for the sea sun,

Hunched in his nest of coats
on a council bench on the cliff.

He is riddled with stares,
picked over by the grins
and asides of the clean world.

For a self-conscious moment
anger flickers his fingers –

He might heave a curse at them, stark
and sudden as a sea-bleached bone,

Protest a pine-brown fist.
Fall from his bench in a fit of rags –

But he endures,
motionless,
his face closed, undecipherable
as an ancient headstone,

His future creeping asleep
like a full dog in a hot yard...

The beach fills with a litter
of bare limbs and torsos.

Pale people come to the benches,
spread takeaways and flab.

He sits, still and black as a dead thing
strung on a keeper's wire.

Youngsters dare who can get closest.

The bikers arrive, slam helmets
on the rails behind him: *ayup pops,
where's yer friggin' surfboard?*

He is oblivious,
warm...

You've seen him on the road
at dusk as you weave the byways
in your suburb-bound saloons:

Clutching his bags to his coat,

Darker than the hump of night
and rook flight homeward.

Old Yeomen

in memoriam

Inoffensive men,
deliberate as gravediggers,
circumspect as peace envoys;

Shy men, with faces like crumpled hillsides,
where they kept clandestine watch
until they trusted you; faces that broke
into a score of sunlit streams
if you spoke of Suffolks or Frisians.

Steady men in humble caps
passing patiently on tractors,
regular as pendulums
to the fields they knew like clan secrets.

Haytime or harvest you could sit with them
in the hedgeback, gulping
unsweetened tea, feeling rooted,
feeling nothing could ever displace you,
that you could become a tree, like them –

A pine maybe, stark with gestures,
or a knotted thorn,
swaying beneath changing skies,
creaking at anchor...

They only wanted enough to cover
the lean years, feeding the rest
back in to the edible furrow.

They only wanted to be what they were:
efficient as midwives in the calf pen,
certain as connoisseurs – tasting,
heads raised to the wind like horses,
the newlaid silver hay…

Tragedy seemed something remote,
like a Middle-Eastern conflict,
but it came, fastened on to them
like a family curse:

A string of wet years, lost contracts,
disease and government bungling,
wore at them like a non-stop bombardment,
stunned them into grim immobility.

They yielded, like bulldozed oaks
shoved aside for a motorway,
letting go of the earth
that would soon bear no trace of them
like a bus terminus…

Self-conscious as boys, they posed for press
on sale day, then faded, like mourners
from a graveside, into exile;
joining the ranks of the obsolete
and curious, like rare breeds of sheep,
or old hand-implements.

They drove out from town now and then,
to brood over strangers' crops
like ancestral ghosts,
leaning on other men's gates,
watching skies
that passed by without them –

Raising their heads in mute wonder,
like horses,
to the winds of an altered world.

Valediction

on the death of my mother

You are so frail:

In the bedroom's half-light
objects stand around you
indifferent as strangers' lives,
insulting your intelligence
in their mundane materiality,

Their obscene mockery
of witless permanence.

I want to smash the room, to show
nothing compared with you
has power to endure...

But dying you are already so strong:

Your resolve towers over me
unfaltering
the only fixed thing on earth.

I am so weak,
almost nothing,
hinged to existence by your stillness...

But I am so vast:

Like the gigantic evening shadow
of some shelled-out frontier fortress
cast on the dusty silence.

Under the silence my loss
slowly becoming you,
your absence becoming me...

Any moment you will be gone:

Homeless,
as if cast out
like an intruder,

Cut adrift
from the welcoming kettle,
from our afternoon chats
on free will and fate...

From the place you cared for
offering succour to others;

Gone –

As if you just called in for a visit
and forgot your scarf and coat,

As if I was merely
a passing acquaintance;

Gone –
Like a waif, to wander
through uncharted worlds,
through parallel
disconcerting realities...

Gone –

Without a proper goodbye,
your dead gaze as if far off, fixed
on distant unknown horizons...

Slipping away
as though you were already
someone else:

An unrecognised figure in a queue
at a separate turnstile.

The Wood Gatherer

My father fought the log, struggled
under a thing numb as a corpse,
as the deadweight of his poverty,
staggered off through the moonlit wood
like a penitent with his burden.

I tried to help with my four-years-old strength,
but tripped in the briars, fell
into an ambush of waiting knives,

Followed him, bleeding,
through the hissing conspiratorial trees,
thorns lashing my bare legs like scourges,
tugging small branches along, like unwilling dogs,
a young hunter determined to bring back a kill;

My first taste of wild nature,
compassionless as an icecap,
exhilarating as desert rain...

We went every night like buccaneers
to raid the plump estates,
but I didn't know why, not then,
that the postwar poor clung like cliff grass
to a fractured and crumbling land,
that peace was just a different battlefield...

My father aged, became shorter,
more affluent and remote
like a visiting dignitary;
preoccupied and lonelier, a man
tied to a desk like a hostage.

Occasionally he remembered me,
invited me on respectable exploits
like walking in the hills;

My father, taller again on those days,
striding through summer air deep
with the scents of peat and moor sheep;
the regenerated raider
in flannel shirt and corduroys...

We stood in the evening sun
radiant as ancient gods,
awaiting the last train into exile.

My father, packing the thermos,
already the loneliest man on earth,
watching the landscape flickering past
like an irretrievable dream of release.

My father, stiffening in the mould
others had cast him in,
hanging on for retirement
like a promised land –

Where the ghost of that old buccaneer
had gone on far ahead,
leaving no tracks behind.

The Lament of Enkidu

1

The trees turned away
as though I was a traitor
leaving me timber and profit
church pews
an obsolete navy
shotgun stocks
and mass-produced roof sections

And the grass burned out its miracle
to a level nonentity
leaving me no choice
but Herefords and steak bars
tarmac
and transcontinental schedules

And the hills humped off
into the annals of extinction
leaving dead grouse
dead foxes
dead settlements
dead sensibilities –
a paradise for flies and necrophiliacs

And I discovered the universe
prayed
made love and got drunk
in the incipient terror of my emptiness

2

Now you are all I have

And this house and our kids and
a good job and my pension policy
and the Volvo and our holidays and
plasma TV and the Sweet Lord Jesus
and my political uncertainties and
my unpredictable erection and –

At night I dream of fabulous lands
where I walk at ease
and my body shimmers

3

I came from the sunrise
to the silent pool in the mountains
not knowing I wanted you

Innocence –
the slumber of the damned

What shall we say to the children?

I came from the sunrise
in simple peace,
selfless incarnation

You were there
in your polyester slacks and plastic anorak
in the sudden image of my insufficiency

Turning away from love
I wanted you and took you
without joy

I slept
I woke
I was reborn alone...

Now I am separate from all things

My reflection in the wasteground puddles
is more connected to the world than I...

4

Are you still there in your darkness?

I am still here in mine,
somewhere…

Soon, soon, we will know where we are
on the long road
we will decipher the signs

We will acknowledge our journey

We will reconnect
like raindrops and tears

Soon, soon...

So eat
drink
and chat up your neighbour's wife
because now, when it happens,
we die

5

Above me stonelips, parted –
the evening's last bliss of waters

Below me the pathways of desire

Above me the wildcat's eye –
its birth-furnace

Below me the sequined limbs of the city
lazing smokily

Above me the artless nakedness of the present

Below me the veil of the future, lifting...

I descend

I stand by the quiet gate in the evening
with my pipe and my memories
my regrets and excuses
and the still-weeping wound of the question:

How far was my fall?

Under my feet the earth.

Above me the sunset.

Words Before Dark

Evening in your room:
spilt shadows,
fingersmears in dust.

We sit
we smoke
we talk…

We balance out across the gulf
of our own dizzy Niagara.

An edgy anecdote. Laughter
like a lifeline falling short…

What are we doing here?
Who will we be by tomorrow?

Can we conjure up a spell
to exorcise this lonely desperation?

Yesterday we met:
a half-glimpsed phantom rose
and vanished in your glance –
I almost had time to believe in it.

Is that why I am here?

Or was it other eyes that watched:
deprivation's eyes in the cave of empty days,
wanting your hair,
your flesh, your smell,
every scrap of you for sustenance?

Have I come here only to steal your life?

Already I begin to dread
what we might do to love…

We sit
we talk
we smoke the endless cigarette of time…

We pace through the museum of the past
searching to disinter some evidence of life,
examining the tombs for light.

I mention the Sixties. You say
love must have gone underground
like the elves –

A rumour now. Folklore.

The evening shadows stain the walls
like ugly incidents. You ask
can we ever save ourselves?

I open wine in place of platitudes.

We press together at the bedroom door,
our bodies swimming deep
in an embrace beyond desire…

Later we lie and listen
to the wind beyond the glass,
the wind that brings the world back
from the other side of time.

You say, I see there are two deaths.

And would this death be love?

The Escapist

My brother was running…

It was the faces he saw that he fled from:

The greeting faces of his neighbours
where the snipers slipped into hiding

The business faces at the tables
adjusting their sleepless self-interest
and their reputations

The face alone in the mirror
like the last face on earth –
the face-upwards-face, floating
on the moor-tarn of dread in the mind…

He ran from the grinning freaks on the cereal pack
that had kidnapped his children,
from the faces of officials
sinister-blank as radar scanners

He reached for his wife, but her face
had flown into deep space –
she was fleeing his fleeing,
she was faceless

He sought the parchment-calm of the priest,
who unleashed guilt and shame
and judgement on his heels
like a hell-horde

and he fled
fled
fled from them

He fled from the face of the suicide
that called him to stop…

He turned from them all,
fearing them, hating them,
the faces without love he was stuck with –
the masks of a brother's face

My brother, who ran in my legs,
woke in my nights
spoke in my blood,
urgent
urgent
for me to follow…

My brother, who wanted
to run from his running,
to run himself into oblivion
like a man wanting to die

To run himself into eternity –

like a man wanting to live

The Passion

In hedgeside and treeline
it is already night.

A flood of low mist hushes the valley;
Charolais at rest on the hill
become phantoms of memory.

In the room only the flickering
of thoughts that do not want to die;
only the drip of the broken tap
like an echo of the drumming pulse
like frantic insistent fingers…

*

Do you remember walking through ripe cornfields
white as Saharan sands, walking
toward the sunrise, as though
you had no other home but light?

And the gull, unannounced
as love, high and alone, at rest
in its own perfection,
like a gift for the mind to hold,
speechless?

And the forest skyline rising
in the wind, like the seething hands
of a mob: from horizon to horizon
the ragged anguish of all trapped
and cornered things –
the hollow voice of loss?

*

The lattice of definition will not hold.

I lie under the charred spars
of a gutted house, in the silence
behind the dust-veils of the collapsing centuries.

The survival-pack of language has almost gone...

I have returned from the years of journeys
that seemed to have meaning,
with the metaphors of pain
clogging my throat like soot.

*

In the room only the ache
of something that cannot speak –
an unreachable beseeching hand;

Only the slow seepage from a leaking drain
like the sidling hiss of betrayal...

On ridge and headland
it is unruffled night.

The heron, like a lake-depth darkness,
lifts in silhouette
and the eyes of the waters close.

Dusk

The black arête of the distant forest
has become a blue plateau.

Sheep in the hill field
are an outcrop of Pliocene boulders.

Temperature drops. Birds turn
to metal on their perches.

There is a sense of the air drying out,
a crackle of static
as water locks into ice.

In the silence I hear clumps
of couch grass stiffening
as if their brittle skeletons are reassembling...

Eaten to bone by snowbound rabbits
a fallen ash branch glimmers towards me –

It is so pale it will point always into darkness.

Mad Grimshaw

Drawn to laughter like an incubus
to flesh, he came, with orgasmic rage,
to smash their violins, to hammer
Thou shalt not!
into every wayward brain.

Red-faced as a demon, he flapped
over the windy moors, ejaculating
the acrid viscum of his wrath –
Thou shalt not!

Behind him the towers
of the new industrial tyranny
sprang up like giant phalli
from the stripped subjected earth...

In the lonely parsonage night
crept in like the Tempter's breath.
Don't touch! God, unforgiving
as the crags of millstone grit,
can see beneath the sheets!

They fell before him
in the Haworth church,
submissive at last,
saved by their shame –
Thou shalt not!

Ready for work,
prepared for slavery.

The Existentialist

Still it continues:

cataracts of may blossom

gnat columns swirling like dust devils

the deep woods foaming into leaf
boiling through midsummer

birdsong –
the spilled riches…

Still it continues:

not intensity of perception, but eyes
behind glass: drowned eyes
in the dentist's aquarium

thought only –
the chained penitents of the past –
and terror of its insufficiency…

Still it continues:

you and me on our separate horizons,
like abandoned monuments
of someone else's folly:

the ruins others have made of us –
debris of civilisations…

Still it continues:

not the self-erasing laughter
of the old man under the baobab

but flight from the mind's silence
in the suburban kitchen's desert immensity...

But not flight either:

the nails through the hands and feet;

the willow stake driven through the heart.

Devils

after Norman Cohn

Under northern skies
pale as a bishop's belly
I walk through the filthy drizzle
of a European summer...

And here they are again,
a fresh crop of dead things
hanging in the elder tree:

Squirrels,
weasels,
jays...

The gamekeepers have strung up their mothers –
the dark gods of the light
behind the mask of the functionary.

Wind-ravened,
weather-emptied,
the hollow fruits of persecution sway
like victims of the vehmgericht:

Graff Grunenberg bobbing
like a dancing doll
from the sacred limes at Lichtenfels...

Pagans,
witches,
heretics:

The enemies of church and state
charred blobs,
small heaps of bones,
in the hellfires' infernal smoulderings...

But they keep coming,
as though the flames had renewed them,
like some dying and reborn deity:

Negroes,
gypsies,
Jews...

Changing with the age like shapeshifters,
teeming, as if deathless,
from the fevered dreams of officialdom:

Homosexuals,
dissident poets,
anti-capitalist protesters –

Pouring, like liberated spirits,
through the cracking damwalls of consciousness...

Then, certain as sunset, the solution:

The executioners, released
from the straightjackets of church and state –

The ones with the guns
and tanks and fixed stares...

Those dark gods of the light
with their specialist techniques
and their orders.

1961

They melted away like spectres
at sunrise, like witches
from a world of implanted fears,
to lie invisible
in the unshorn grass
beyond the hockey fields'
docile conformity.

Smoking was the illicit thrill at first:
the sensuality of cigarettes –
touching fingers,
lips – releasing
deeper whispers
whisked away on the tousling wind.

Until a day of summer stillness,
listless, swamp humid,
sparked an eerie electricity:
flickering thunderlight above the fields,
fevered currents in the blood –

and a new identity burst,
like a submerged island,
through the stagnant scum of consensus...

Like secret agents
their double life began:
pariahs in the shadows
poised, like opportunist thieves,
to steal moments
from the rule-bound world.

Incendiary glances in the classrooms
burned through the dusty air,
consuming oxygen like a bush fire,
leaving them breathless,

impatient to escape
to their private island –

hoping no search parties were out,
closing in, like proselytizing priests,
to bind and to exorcise
with their spells of guilt and shame.

Drover

February afternoon: the sky
white as the sands of Morar,
the north wind sneaking
through the outlying streets
like the scouts of a border raiding band.

Dougal watched the market crowds
thinning, as though Charlie hissel
was at the gates, heard five strokes
chime in the Norman tower – a summons
to lardy Saxon wives and firesides.

Dung caked and dusty
the cattle pens were empty,
except for a few beasts, louring
like sullen prisoners through their bars.

But there was a moment here
to seize, like a dropped coin
glegged i' the mud – a chance
for an old highland drover to keep
hissel in meat another week...

Dougal had done *the lang Scots miles*
bringing the big herds down,
bucking and bobbing,
like a frothing sea off Knoydart,
down from the northern glens
to the soft-bellied Saxon shires.

Lame now from the ten-years-old kick
of the tinker's wall-eyed nag,
he was washed up like a beached skiff
no-one has use for, dried out
under drear English skies
and fearing the workhouse –
an outsider still among close-bred Saxons.

He wanted to wake in the heather,
the beasts, placid as just-born calves,
steaming and belching around him
and eat the smoke-dried meat
from his belt, feeling the wind's
clean chill from Sgurr Nan Gillean.

But there was no work for a drover
who hobbled no faster
than keening crones to a burial...

Reeking of sweat and horse muck
The Fleece was packed as a riot:
stockmen and drovers telling
their tales of the past days –
who'd lost his shirt at the races,
who'd lost sheep to the tinkers;

Brawny farmers, in best boots
and worsteds, draining a last jug,
or two if they'd won their joins.

Dougal surged in with a thirst
for work that a serious drinker
has for ale – and he was lucky:
the penned beasts were to go
to Abe Tate, the tenant at Cobdale.

By now the drovers were drunk
in the snug and leery, fearing
travellers' talk of snow in the wind
and not a man rose to the challenge.

Big Alf Budge saved face for them all:
Thoo wants ti tek 'em Dougie,
they'll put thoo up at Cobdeall!

Dougal saw the looks and winks,
the nods and smiles – but damn,
he'd done the Pennine miles!
and this was only twenty – so
he palmed the agent's coins and left...

Night swept in like a treacherous tide
as Dougal climbed the scarp edge
of the Wolds, the beasts surging ahead,
wanting shelter, catching fear
from each other like a pox, picking up
the whiff of snow in the wind.

If he'd had the gift he'd have summoned
a kelpie, called her up from the boggy ponds
to gallop and guide him
through the thickening night,
but he wasna sure if Saxon ponds
held more than mucky watter.

At Tate's no bed was offered,
no warm crisp straw in barn
or roaring saddle room,
but the big dull-eyed foreman
put more coins in his outstretched hand –
and Dougal, like a rumour, was gone...

The snow caught him with six miles to go:
a blizzard thick as blown chaff
at a threshing; stumbling
and winded he lay up in a chalk pit
a mile from the scarp edge
and the climb down to safety.

The drifting snow piled around him
in fluffy pillows and quilts,
softer he thought and cleaner
than a bed in the workhouse.

He waited for a lull and slept,
dreamed he was back in the glens
of Druim Fada, taking the beasts
down Glen Loy to Gairlochy,
or wandering through Glen Shiel,
hearing the wild cats' cries
in the pines by Loch Duich.

And it seemed at a whim he was there
by the lochside, with the wee sheltie
he'd had once bouncing towards him;
not lame, with a fresh westerly at his back
lengthening his strides like a laddie,
loping the lang Kintail shielings together...

They found him a week later
after the thaw, the double pay
in his pocket they used
to send him back to Knoydart.

The Saxon drovers in the snugs
laughed at the tale on snowy nights,
calling the chalk pit *Dougal's Folly,*
the youngest among them agog
that an old bobbing Scot
could do something so risky.

But hasna a Saxon ever feared death
among strangers in a foreign workhouse?

Feeding Time

All cloudless September the bullocks have stood
in the stifling shut-in twilight.

I open the feed-house door
and a gated-off tonnage of beef
surfaces towards me: a looming school
of sexless simpletons, sacrifices
to the market's Transylvanian blood lust.

I enter their pen with the barley –
they press their soft gaze to the bars,
drooling threadbare curtains of saliva
in their infantile anticipation.

As I fill the feed-troughs
they are a brief stampede
of colossal imbeciles, jostling
hugely in vacuous timid excitement.

Like an omnipotent king
I watch over my subjects,
docile as day-old calves
behind the contented emptiness of their eyes.

I fasten them in and leave them
in their gigantic impotence, knowing
in three weeks they will be gone
and I will remain.

Primal

for Ray

I plunged out with a storm lamp,
leaned into the heaving gale
that came at me like the force
of a sorcerer's intent, battled
to the dark barn to find the calf
stuck as a blocked sump,
only six inches of legs showing
like a promise denied.

It had been like this they said
for half an hour, so the three of us
roped the legs and pulled, leaning back
in the straw like a tug-of-war team,
as if tied to a fate we could not escape
in the manic goblin dance
of wind-woken shadows.

Then I saw him, an arm's reach away:
almost a ton of ghost-pale Charolais bull,
one red eye watching us, the other
fixed on the clattering woodwork
of the wind-spooked barn,
a Cretaceous boulder
of colossal geological stillness.

They had brought him in to be with her,
that his impassive presence
might reassure the worn-out cow,
his burning red stare a beam
of life energy, an emission
from the furnace of shape and form,
the dwarf forge of beginnings.

He lay there, his thick power-lifter's legs
neatly folded, at rest by my elbow
silent and still as a waiting landmine,
while we hauled like madmen,
trying to drag life back from an abyss
as if it was pulling against us,
the calf reluctant to leave
the pain-free pre-birth world.

One tectonic twitch
of the bull's sedimentary shoulder
and the calf could be on its way
at a gallop to the steak bar,
but he preferred to observe,
as if letting us work for him,
like feudal serfs for their overlord.

After nearly an hour we got him,
slithering out almost like an afterthought,
the lamplight bouncing
from two new eyes
filled with passive birth-sadness,
while we, groggy with effort,
watched the primaeval
all-mother licking ritual click in...

With swelling subterranean rumblings
the bull arose, compelling
as a resurgent legend,
shaking his head as though flinging off
generations of subservience,
quietly breathing in his creation,
then with triumphal fanfare
bellowing acknowledgement – *That's my lad!*

Hunt

With their cleanshaven faces and privileged profiles
the horsemen are riding out of their picture frame
down from the mantelpiece…

They arrive in the field
at an arrogant canter –

And the fox is off through the blazing grasses
and the hounds are plunging after their voices
and the horsemen are galloping full tilt
galloping
galloping
trying to get to the present

High in the oaktop the woodpecker laughs
like a skull in a nightmare –
he knows they won't make it…

The hounds are deep in the beeches
shaking rabbits like doormats
tossing the bodies between them
like a basketball warm-up

And the horsemen are galloping breakneck
galloping
galloping
but the past is too long
for them to ride free from…

The hounds are turning away
to ravage the rest of the county
to roll on its carcase and pick up its parasites

And the horsemen are lost in the boggy meadow
hung on the wall
between mask-gapes and antlers...

Miles away
and years later
the tumbled rocks on a hillside
are brushed briefly
by the elusive whiff of fox.

Jack of Hearts

a tale of (attempted) murder

Listen –

The drone of pigeons from the evening woods
like a hidden engine idling…

Listen –

A new note, like traffic on a distant motorway,
an insistent muffled frenzy…

Flies!

Meat flies,
the big flies of Sabra and Shatila –

There's a death,
wide-eyed as a child,
in the woodside.

Jack's about…

*

See him –

In the yellow-eyed twilight of December afternoons
stuffing overfed pheasants into a sack…

See him –

Jack in his pin-stripes,
the best dressed poacher in the county –
a serious joke, like authority.

Poor Jack, in his dead dad's Sunday best
and his charity shop shirt;

Rich Jack, feasting like Falstaff, doing his own
politically incorrect thing, like the weather;

Setting his snares in the muddy runs of our minds
to catch our grotesque denials.

*

The whispers began,
like drizzle upon dry pastures:

Jack the anarchist, Jack the thief,
Jack can cast spells in your handkerchief,
like the first germs of an epidemic;

Jack the terrorist, Jack the spy,
Jack has the curse of the evil eye;

Jack-beneath-the-pillow,
pulling the strings of our fears,
opening us up like a truth serum…

Subliminal whispers
hanging in the wind
like the dust of a divided land.

*

Listen:

The drone of pigeons from the evening woods
is silent –

Listen:

A dirge of meat flies,
the big flies of the secret body dumps –

There's a death,
open-mouthed as a babe,
in the woodside…

Who is it lying still as a tripwire
as Baghdad debris
under the hawthorns?

A smart lad in pin-stripes…

*

But they won't die, those renegade spirits,
the bullet, the noose,
the poisoned cup can't quell them;

They stalk us, home in
unerring as flies
on our expedient slaughter.

Listen:
Jack's about…

Jack the avenger –
invading our nights, our waking reveries,
aiming our own gun barrels
at the space between our eyes.

Kill him! Kill him!
Kill him if you can…

Or follow him. Offer him your heart.

Derwent Ings

There were goblins here back then;
gone now, pressed flat as cartoon cats
against the back wall of RJB's mine.

We wouldn't see them anyway
if they came bounding out
to girn and gape at us.

The energy fields won't sustain them...

In a landscape that was once
more charged, the worlds
were closer, indivisible as air.

*

The old priory lies quiet
as a forgotten graveyard
in its field of bumpy grass.

God, with nowhere to go,
melted into the mists
like a tantalising rumour.

The power down here was always
the river: the Celts' twice-sacred
river of oaks; a giver of riches,
a brown and sinewy mystery.

*

In the bushes the last birdsong
threads daylight and darkness together.

Geese home in from their feeding grounds,
their wild calls carving a flightpath through the dusk.

Curlews bubble like marsh spirits
and the wind shrieks
like a keening spectre in the reeds.

Beneath it all the big subliminal
base drum of the river
booms softly, like a heart.

*

Shards and splinters, chunks
of shattered moon in the rushes:
beguiling will-o'-the-wisps,
quivering faery lanterns
so deep in the otherworld
we will never reach them.

Grass under the flood
like drowned hair –
the world of the dead
rising to meet us.

*

Water, riffled by breezes
or owl breath,
spread as far as horizon warning stars.

The ebb and flow, the rise
and fall of the flood-meadows,
like the tide
and the planet breathing.

The river, the deep pulse
of the earth's blood:

The mighty throbbing engine that drives the land.

Goodmanham

1

Spirit paths and 4×4s;
earth energies and SSSIs –
we are here, now
and in England:

Parallel realities
joined leaf and flame
like two sides of a sacred tree.

2

The village elderly have lost their memories.
The threadbare cloak of folk tradition:

Patched-up intimations
of a one-time wondrous robe…

There are no fairies in the hill,
but UFOs hover
round the microwave tower.

3

All Hallows on its Neolithic mound.

Samhain eve and the ghosts
of the dead rise up
to crouch beside the digital screens.

Plato's advice to invaders
and Gregory's to Augustine:
preserve the shrine, but change the deities.

4

A high priest's dubious apostasy:
the war axe flung into the sanctuary.

Saxon pagandom degenerate?
Christianity embraced to outface Paulinus?
A priest's spur: retention of familiar authority...

And Edwin, to secure his crown, requiring
a Kentish though a Christian bride.

5

This king, convinced by an auspicious trinity:
an abortive knife assault, a battle victory,
a royal daughter's birth,
espoused the faith and annexed Kent.

Such are the persuasions of ambitious men...

The Saxon font remains
at the west end of the Norman nave.

6

Arcane knowledge flows between architrave and arch:

Secrets secure from uninitiated men;
outliving desperate kings and purblind governments –
the geometry of cosmic harmony in stone.

Straight as inspiration the unseen pulse was set:
the subtle powers of sun and moon
waking the mystery of the inmost earth.

Galtres

remains of an ancient forest

Robin Hood was at home here,
of course, till the diligent Victorians
erased him from the corbel tables.

Like the last remnants
of some unimaginable exodus,
birches straggle by the golf course fence
as though stuck in a time warp.

Large stands are few now,
anachronistic and beleaguered,
marooned in an ocean of progress.

A million birds sang up the sun here
like the perpetual choirs of Albion
and the quicksilver earth spirit
ran feral and unfettered.

Aeons of mystery replaced
by MOD ranges, a bypass, a maze
of new estates – the private paradise
of the Englishman's garden...

But there is still a lingering otherness:
a sense of ancient presences
in forgotten corners, as if unseen eyes
looked back at us
in reproach or valediction...

Just an illusion, of course.

The way leaves swirl in the wind
is no longer the Green Man dancing,
but a false folk-memory, a trick of the light.

On Bella Hill

a poem for celebrants

Moon-stilled, the afternoon winds
have merged with the spellbound earth.

Familiarity fades from valley-head and hollow
like the used-up ideas of a life.

Reich would have noticed the orgone
darkening, the thickening breath of night,
like the exhalation of some enchanted beast,
masking the learned world.

An eerie call, like awakened memories
of the *bean shidh*'s wail,
sends consciousness reeling
like a shellburst…

Is this the world of nightbirds or spirits?

This is the time when the adept steps
from the mists at Gorsedd Arberth,

When the worlds shudder apart
from the stars
to the deepest dream of earth…

Other truths, other realities,
mingling like smoke rings,
like links in a faery chain,

Taking us beyond
our self-imposed limitations
to other times, other places,
whose voices we have not yet recalled.

Those Old Reunions

In the cloakroom the empty coats wait
like a row of abandoned souls.

Around the tables the conversations
run neck and neck
with the duration of hidden pain.

Silence too keeps pace
like a patient assassin...

Beyond the glass owlflight
arcs through forecourt lights
like a swiping blade.

Someone is standing, following
the drink's tray: hoping,
after so many years, his knees,
like trusted friends, don't betray him.

Silence follows like a doppelganger...

Outside, the lawn-edge woods
steadily fill with blood.

Someone is leaving, stepping
into the streaming darkness,
trying to wade out to an iceberg –

Behind him the house,
the lights, the anecdotes
have faded into the album...

Thirty a decade back
now only twelve:

But still the grins persist
on page after page,
like an insurance premium
their owners are too fearful not to pay.

Lines In Early Winter

Like spectres of a doomed platoon
they rise to meet me from the night,

Like the dead at Samhain out on parole.

Umbellifers by the woodside fence:
a skeletal grisaille, cupping their snow like gifts.

They hold it aloft like trophies,
like mementos of death.

Behind them the stream chatters its tray of wineglasses...

Their dead arms are raised in a toast
to those, perhaps, who will listen,

For the whispers, the lost songs
the unacknowledged voices from the past,

Revealing the paths we have trodden,
the footfalls that lead to our own doors.

Notes

High Intake
This poem is loosely based on an old tale from the North York Moors.

When Beasts Most Graze
Records exist of over 2000 settlements which today are reduced to grassy mounds. They were deserted during the 14th and 15th centuries, mainly due to the change from mixed farming to the exclusive raising of sheep for wool and for the landowners' profits.

Ironstone Miners, 1874
In the nineteenth century the North Yorkshire settlement of Rosedale was the centre of a large-scale ironstone mining operation. The work was unremittingly hard, dangerous and badly paid.

Blackamore
Blackamore is the old name for the North York Moors.

Years
The Rev. J.B. Schorey, curate of Scrayingham, died in York Lunatic Asylum on 10 December 1812, aged 41. He had been robbed of his possessions by Asylum officials and, like an unknown number of patients in that institution, may have been systematically starved to death.

The Lament of Enkidu
Enkidu is a character in the epic poem *Gilgamesh*.

Mad Grimshaw
William Grimshaw, known to some as the 'flogging preacher' and 'Mad Grimshaw', was rector of Haworth from 1742 until his death in 1763.

1961

The decriminalisation of same-sex sexual activity did not occur until 1967 in England and Wales, 1981 in Scotland and 1982 in Northern Ireland.

Drover

A 'join' was a cash bet on the sale price of an animal auctioned at market.

Derwent Ings

'Ings' is the old Norse word for a water meadow.

Galtres

Claimed for exclusive royal hunting use by the Norman kings of England, Galtres Forest lay to the north and north-east of the city of York. However, the forest was already ancient by the time the Normans arrived with their brutal forest laws and was until then open to all the local people.

On Bella Hill

This poem is a meditation on the sacred Celtic quarter-day of *Samhain*.

Acknowledgements

Thanks are due to the editors of the following publications, in whose pages some of these poems first appeared: *Agenda, Anglo-Welsh Review, Encounter, Envoi, Green's Magazine, Green River Review, London Magazine, New Poetry, New Yorkshire Writing, Oasis, Poetry & Audience, Poetry Matters, Poetry Review, Stand, Thames Poetry, The Present Tense, The Sewanee Review, Tribune, Turbulence, Yorkshire Review.*

'When Beasts Most Graze' won first prize in the 1975 Stroud Festival International Poetry Competition. 'Years' was the winner of the Poetry Society's 1977 Greenwood Prize. 'The Passion' was published in a numbered pamphlet series by Sceptre Press in 1979. *Hunt* was broadcast on Poetry Now (BBC Radio 3).

Some of these poems were first published by Peterloo in *The Hollow Places* (1980) and *Killers* (1984).